LAO FOLKTALES

STEVEN JAY EPSTEIN

T0344243

Silkworm Books

ISBN: 978-974-9575-87-1

This edition is published in 2005 by
Silkworm Books
430/58 Soi Ratchaphruek, M. 7, T. Mae Hia,
A. Mueang Chiang Mai, Thailand 50100
info@silkwormbooks.com
http://www.silkwormbooks.com

Typeset in 10 pt. Warnock Pro by Silk Type

CONTENTS

INTRODUCTION

I moved to Vientiane, the capital of the People's Democratic Republic of Laos, in December of 1990. It was a small, leisurely, uncrowded city. Boys and girls on bicycles two-by-two chatted and giggled and flirted, making way for an occasional four-wheel drive vehicle of an international organization or an embassy. The streets were deserted at noon. Vientiane was the place where I mastered the art of the nap.

The Lao socialized in the seasonal rounds of Buddhist temple ceremonies, weddings, housewarmings, and baby welcomings. Most foreigners hung out at the post-colonial Australian Club which barred Lao membership but had a cool pool with a panoramic view of the Mekong River.

There was little to do at night. I spent the evenings chatting with friends, drinking Beer Lao, and batting away mosquitoes. No one I knew watched television. There were few television sets. Those that did exist were tuned, by government edict, to the national television station which presented public service programs highlighting the achievements of the People's Government campaigns with an emphasis on the rice production in specific provinces.

I lived in a small two-bedroom house overlooking a rice field. One hot humid evening I wandered up my lane to find a small crowd gathered on the broad veranda of my neighbor's house. They were listening to Uncle Phut, a twinkly round-bellied figure with a fondness for alcohol, telling a story. Uncle Phut had my neighbors laughing, cackling, and chortling. With typical warm Lao hospitality, I was invited over, offered the most comfortable chair and given a glass of cool water flavored with whiskey. I understood little, except when Uncle Phut would wink at me and say, with an exaggerated mock foreign accent, "Mis-tah Sa-teep." This would incite another round of laughter. I had been given a minor (and my informant assured me, not unflattering) role in his tale.

Months later I was studying the Lao language and I asked my teacher to spice up the lessons with some Lao stories. That is when I first met up with Xieng Mieng. The first Xieng Mieng tale I heard was "What's in the Bamboo Tube?" I was hooked for life. I pestered my Lao friends and colleagues to share these tales. Soon I had collected a stack of Lao folktales.

Many of the tales with animal themes have their roots in the Panchatantra and Jataka tales. The Panchatantra tales originated in India about twenty-three hundred years ago. The story is told that long ago there was a king who was dissatisfied with the schooling of his children. He hired a wise man to be their teacher. The wise man taught the children stories to improve their moral development. The Panchatantra tales are the basis for Aesop's fables. The Jataka tales are a collection of stories of the past lives of the Buddha. In the Buddha's previous incarnations, he took many forms, some animal and some human. There is a significant overlap between the Panchatantra and Jataka tales.

I used these tales in my English classes as teaching materials. They were wildly successful and popular. I decided that these tales needed a wider audience and determined to get them published. I tracked down Mr. Anoulom Souvandouane who is regarded as Laos' premiere illustrator. I enlisted his support and we spent many happy hours in his cramped studio on Phonkheng Road discussing the tales and trying to match the illustrations to the stories. Finally, with the considerable assistance of Somsanouk Mixay, the editor of *The Vientiane Times*, we managed to get these books published.

Folktales are not static. Just as Uncle Phut tossed me into his telling of his tale, storytellers reweave the tales, pulling the audience into its warp and woof. The tales are tailored and refashioned for the audience. Local characters, customs, settings and details are added to make the tale more familiar, more topical, and, usually, funnier. The storyteller often adds his own agenda to the tale. I have honored this tradition by sneaking in occasional health and environmental messages, plugging the nascent Lao coffee industry, naming some characters for my Lao friends, and spicing up the humor.

I heard these tales in a specific historical context. The victory of the Communist Pathet Lao over the United States-backed royalist regime was still fresh in people's minds. The versions of the popular Lao folktales that I heard were shaped by the propaganda of the Pathet Lao. It is easy to see how these tales were used by the Pathet Lao in their struggle to defeat the wealthier and better-armed royalist troops. "Speed vs. Cunning" is a metaphor for how the Pathet Lao envisioned how their superior organization and strategy could overcome their better-armed and better-financed enemy. Xieng Mieng represents the common man and his struggle against the bourgeoisie and the monarchy. One can imagine these stories being told in the Pathet Lao headquarters in the caves of Sam Neua province while American planes dropped bombs overhead.

When my Lao colleagues read this introduction I know that they will say: "Steve, you are taking this much too seriously."

These tales may have been used to encourage the revolutionary forces but they were also used to entertain. Foreigners living in Laos are struck by the constant good humor of the Lao. They love a good laugh. Having a good time is a high priority. Life is not to be taken too seriously.

When you read these tales I hope that you will get a taste of this Lao humor.

ACKNOWLEDGMENTS

The author would like to thank the many storytellers who shared their time, knowledge, and humor: Dr. Arthur Crisfield, Amphay Chitmanoh, Xayleusa Phouyavong, Khanthavone, Somvone Siamphay, Thavisak Sunnapa, Suvath Douangta, Vanthong Saykhampheth, Bountha Songyerthao, Khamsouk Phommapath, Khamphanh Luangamath, Sivath Sengdouangchanh, Khampasong Ratsachack, Khounsouvanh, Khampheng Soundara, Phaiwan Keovilay, Somkhuanta Souvanthalisith, Hengnakhone Keovisien, Sengthong Photisan, Anoulom Souvandouane, Kysinh Sinhpanngam, Phra Bounthavy Inthanam, Phra Somsy Keokhamphone, and Champa Rattanasouvannaphone.

The author gratefully acknowledges the assistance and support of the Lao Ministry of Information and Culture, particularly Somsanuk Mixay of the *Vientiane Times*, Khamseng Soundara, Chanhmali Vannaboun, and Dr. Chanthaphilith Chiemsisouraj.

XIENG MIENG FOLLOWS
THE KING EXACTLY

In the days long ago, before there was television and entertainment meant listening to tales such as these, many Lao people enjoyed chewing betel nut. Chewing betel is not like chewing a stick of gum where you just peel off the wrapper and pop it in your mouth. Betel has to be prepared with special ingredients and special tools that were all kept in a betel basket. And if you were a king you had intricately carved silver tools and a beautifully woven basket carried for you by your betel basket bearer.

"Xieng Mieng," said the king, "today I am going to the horse races. You will carry my betel nut basket and follow me."

"How will we get there?" asked Xieng Mieng.

"I will ride my beautiful white horse and you, Xieng Mieng, will follow me on foot."

"Yes, I will follow you," said Xieng Mieng.

"Exactly," said the king.

The king rode and Xieng Mieng walked out through the gates of the palace, and through the rice fields.

The king rode very fast because his horse was quite strong and speedy. Xieng Mieng walked very slowly because he enjoyed smelling the flowers along the path and sitting in the shade of the broad trees. He even took a bit of a nap.

The king arrived at the horse races. He watched the first race. He watched the second race. He wanted to chew his betel nut. He watched the third race. He watched the fourth race. He *really* wanted to chew his betel nut. He watched the fifth and sixth race. But Xieng Mieng had still not arrived. He watched the seventh and eight race. He was watching the ninth and final race when Xieng Mieng arrived with the betel nut basket.

"Xieng Mieng! Where have you been? I have been waiting for my betel nut basket."

"I am sorry, Your Majesty. You told me to follow you. I followed you. Here I am."

The king remembered his words. "You are right, Xieng Mieng. I did say, 'follow.' Next week I will be going to the races. Next week you will carry my betel basket and you must follow me as quickly as possible. Do you understand?"

"Yes," said Xieng Mieng, "I will follow you as quickly as possible."

"Exactly," said the king.

The following week, the king mounted his beautiful white horse and rode to the races. Xieng Mieng followed as quickly as possible. He ran and ran. He ran so fast that the basket tipped over and the betel nut fell out.

Xieng Mieng stopped for a moment to pick up the betel nut but then he broke into a smile and continued running behind the king.

The king was watching the first horse race when Xieng Mieng, out of breath, came running up the steps.

"Very good, Xieng Mieng. I see that you came as quickly as possible. Now hand me my betel basket."

The king reached into his betel basket.

"There is no betel nut. Where is my betel nut?"

"I dropped it."

"You dropped it? You dropped it? Then why did you not pick it up, you fool?"

"Because, Your Majesty, you said to follow you as quickly as possible. If I stopped to pick up the betel nut I would be late."

The king remembered his words. "You are right, Xieng Mieng. I did say 'follow me as quickly as possible.' Next week I will be going to the races again. Next week you will carry my betel basket and you must follow me as quickly as possible but you must pick up everything that drops. Do you understand?"

"Yes," said Xieng Mieng, "I will follow you as quickly as possible and pick up everything that drops."

"Exactly," said the king.

The next week the king rode on his beautiful white horse to the races and Xieng Mieng followed as quickly as possible with the king's betel basket.

Sure enough, the betel basket tipped over and the betel spilled all over the ground.

Xieng Mieng stopped and collected the betel and put it back in the basket. Xieng Mieng ran to catch up with the king.

He noticed that steaming mounds of manure were plopping and dropping from the horse's backside.

Xieng Mieng smiled. He picked up the manure and put it in the betel basket. More manure dropped and Xieng Mieng collected it all and put it in the betel basket.

In the middle of the second race, Xieng Mieng arrived at the horse races.

"Xieng Mieng, I don't wish to be disappointed. Is there betel in my basket?"

"There is indeed, Your Majesty."

The king reached into the basket for his betel but he grabbed a warm handful of manure.

"What is this? This is manure!"

"Exactly," replied Xieng Mieng.

"And why is there manure in my betel basket?"

"Don't you remember your words, Your Majesty? You said to follow you as quickly as possible and pick up everything that drops. The betel nut dropped. I picked it up. The manure dropped. I picked it up. I followed your words exactly."

THE TRAGIC TALE OF THE FLYING TURTLE

A long time ago there was a beautiful pond filled with fresh clean water. Many birds and fish and animals lived in that pond including a big fat turtle and his best friends, two brother swans. Each morning the swans and the turtle sat and chatted over a cup of coffee at the Pond Coffee Shop.

One year there was a terrible drought. There was very little rain. The rivers and streams that flowed into the pond dried up. And because the rivers and streamed dried up, the pond became smaller and smaller.

One morning the turtle and the swans met as usual at the Pond Coffee Shop but this time they were not drinking coffee. There simply wasn't enough water to make coffee.

"Mr. Turtle, you are our good friend. We have some-thing to tell you. We are moving to a new pond. My brother and I flew all over this land and found a nice new pond. The pond has lots of water and there are many other turtles and swans to play with. We want you to come with us."

"How far is it?"

"About ten minutes as the crow flies."

"About ten minutes as the crow flies is about five months as the turtle walks."

"Yes, that is true. But we have an idea."

The swans smiled and laughed and would have clapped their hands if swans had hands to clap but they flapped their wings instead because they had thought of something quite clever.

"We have a wonderful idea. We will take you with us. You will fly with us!"

"Fly? How can I fly? We turtles have no wings. Who ever heard of a flying turtle?"

But the thought of flying excited the turtle. "I would like to fly through the air, fly through the clouds, free as a bird. Flying would be wonderful!"

"Here is our plan," continued the swan. "My brother and I will bring a long stick. You will bite the stick in the middle. We will carry the sticks in our beaks. Then we will flap our wings and fly to our new pond. We will carry you through the air. Isn't this a wonderful idea?"

"Do you mean I will fly?" asked the turtle.

"Fly? Well, yes, I guess you will fly. It will be fun. You aren't afraid, are you?"

"Afraid? Turtles are afraid of nothing." And the turtle again thought about flying through the air, free as a bird.

"Now, Mr. Turtle, please listen because this is very important. You must not open your mouth. Do you understand?"

"No problem."

The swans brought the stick. Each swan held the stick in its beak. The turtle walked between the swans and took hold of the stick with its mouth. The swans checked the turtle's grip on the stick, gave each other a wink, flapped their wings, and flew up up up into the sky.

"This is wonderful," thought the turtle. "I am really flying! Look at those trees. How small they are. And the pond looks like a little puddle. And there is a village and some children."

And there *were* children. There was a young boy and a young girl, Phaiwan and Phetmany, playing in their garden.

"I think it might rain today," said Phaiwan looking at the clouds. "Hey! Look at that! There are two swans and a turtle flying through the air!"

"That turtle is carrying the swans!"

"No, Phetmany, turtles cannot fly. The swans are carrying the turtle."

"Phaiwan, I can see with my own eyes, the turtle is carrying the swans."

"Phetmany, turtles don't have wings. They can't fly. The two swans are carrying the turtle."

"No! The turtle is carrying the swan!"

"No! The swans are carrying the turtle!"

The children yelled so loudly that the turtle heard them.

"The girl thinks that the swans are carrying me," thought the turtle. "But I can fly! I am flying now! I am carrying the swans! Yes, I am flying and I am carrying the swans. No, the swans are not carrying me. I am carrying the swans."

"Phaiwan, I know that I am right. The swans are carrying the turtle."

Phaiwan pointed at the three creatures flying above them. "Look, Phetmany, the swans are carrying the turtle."

"No . . . no . . . no . . . no . . . no . . ." yelled the turtle.

The turtle had opened his mouth. He plunged down, down, down through the sky, through the clouds, through the trees to the ground below.

Right next to Phaiwan.

Splat!

The turtle fell from so far and from so high that the crash of the turtle to the ground caused the turtle to explode! And turtle blood and turtle juice sprayed all over Phaiwan's underarm which had been pointing to the sky.

"Oooh! That smells awful," said Phetmany.

"Yecch! It stinks!"

Phaiwan ran to the river to wash off the muck from his underarm.

He washed it once but it still smelled.

Phetmany brought him some soap and he washed it again.

But it still smelled.

He washed it a third time but his underarm still smelled of turtle.

He washed it a fourth time and a fifth time but it still stank.

He washed and washed but as many times as he washed he could never get rid of the smell of the exploding turtle.

And that is why, to this day, men's underarms smell and (in Laos, at least) women's don't.

IT TASTES SWEET

Kham was a very lazy novice. When the other novices were busy carrying out their many duties, Kham was busy trying to make himself scarce. When the other novices were sitting in meditation, Kham was usually fast asleep.

One day the abbot of the temple set off to visit a monk in a neighboring temple. As he was walking out of the temple gates he spotted Kham sleeping under the broad branches of a banyan tree.

"Wake up, Kham!"

"Huh?"

"Kham, you lazy novice, wake up! I have a task for you. I want you to sweep up all the chicken poop on the grounds of the temple. Use this broom."

"Yes, sir. Sweep up the chicken poop. Yes, sir."

Kham took the broom and began busily sweeping the courtyard but as soon as the abbot had walked down the path and was safely out of view he put down the broom and laid himself down to return to his dream.

And that is how the abbot found Kham when he returned that evening. Kham snoozing in the same spot under the banyan tree with the broom across his chest.

"Kham!"

"Huh?"

"Kham, wake up! You lazy novice! When I left the temple this morning I told you to sweep up all of the chicken poop on the temple grounds. You have been sleeping all this time and the grounds are full of chicken poop. Tomorrow you will sweep up all of the chicken poop. If I find even one piece of chicken poop on the temple grounds I will make you eat it."

The very next morning the abbot was hurrying out the gates of the temple. There was Kham sound asleep on a straw mat under the shade of the tree.

"Kham! Wake up! Get up!"

"Yes, sir."

"Kham, I'll be back tomorrow morning. Today you are going to clean up all the chicken poop. Remember what I told you: if I find even one piece of chicken poop I will make you eat it."

"Yes, sir."

But Kham had an idea.

Into the kitchen he went. He scooped out some palm sugar and heated it over the fire. He took the burnt sugar and fashioned it into a shape—a shape that looked remarkably like chicken poop.

Kham smiled as he filled a whole platter with pieces of burnt palm sugar.

The next morning the abbot returned.

"Welcome back, sir," said Kham. "How was your journey?"

"Fine, thank you. Kham, did you sweep up the chicken poop like you were supposed to do?"

"Oh, I knew I was supposed to do something. I forgot."

"Kham, I am going to teach you a lesson. I told you that if you didn't sweep up all of the chicken poop then you would have to eat it. Kham, you must eat the chicken poop."

Kham picked up a piece of chicken poop and popped it in his mouth. He gritted his teeth. He grimaced.

But then his expression changed. He smiled.

"Hmm," said Kham. "This is not bad. Not bad at all."

He picked up another piece of poop and tasted it.

"Actually, this is quite good."

He picked up another one and ate it.

"Yes, apparently chicken poop is quite sweet." Kham licked his lips.

He picked up more and more pieces of poop and popped them into his mouth and chewed them up.

"Hey, this is excellent food. Would you like to try some?"

"Do you think I am stupid? I don't eat chicken poop," said the abbot, staring at Kham.

"It's up to you. It's really quite good."

Kham continued to pick up chicken poop and gobbled them down with gusto, smacking his lips.

"Are you sure you wouldn't like to try just one bite?"

"Hmmm. Maybe I will try just a bit."

Kham handed the abbot a piece. He brought it to his nose. "Doesn't smell bad."

And the abbot sampled it.

"Not bad at all," said the abbot.

"Here, have another," said Kham.

"I don't mind if I do."

And Kham and the abbot ate piece after piece of the sugary chicken poop until they could eat no more.

"I enjoyed that very much, Kham. I didn't realize that chicken poop could taste so good. Now, Kham, listen carefully. Go sweep up all the chicken poop and put it on a big plate. I will eat it tomorrow morning with my tea."

This time Kham happily swept the temple grounds of all of the chicken poop that he could find.

The next morning, the abbot found Kham sitting under the tree with a big platter full of chicken poop.

"Kham, I see that you swept up the chicken poop just like I told you."

"Yes, I did sir. Here it is."

Kham offered the abbot the platter full of chicken poop, which he had artfully arranged in pleasing patterns.

The abbot took one piece of the chicken poop and began to eat it.

"Blecch! Yecch!" he spluttered and sputtered and spat out the chicken poop. "That tastes terrible!"

"What do you expect?" said Kham. "You are eating chicken poop."

THE BOTTLE OF HONEY

A merchant in the kingdom had built a brand new house. So that this new house would be safe and happy, he invited the monks from Kham's temple to perform the house warming ceremony.

After the ceremony was over, the monks were served a delicious meal and sent on their way back to temple.

"I am certain you will like this," said the merchant. The merchant wanted to show his gratitude and he knew just what to give the abbot: a bottle of honey. The abbot loved honey.

And so did Kham.

A few days later, the abbot was called to a village far away from the temple. He would have to stay there a few days. He was gathering a few things for the trip when he noticed his prized bottle of honey. He would have liked to take the honey on his journey but the abbot knew that just wouldn't be right.

"Kham, I will be gone a few days. Take my bottle of honey and put it at the very back of the very top shelf of the larder. Hide it behind the sacks of sticky rice."

"Of course, you can certainly trust me with this bottle of delicious honey. I will put it up at the very back of the very top shelf in the larder."

Kham dragged out the stepladder and climbed up to the top shelf. He safely deposited the bottle in the very back of the shelf, far from view and far from temptation.

The next morning Kham had a thought: "I wonder if that bottle of honey is still there? Maybe a thief came in the middle of the night and stole the honey? I must check."

So Kham dragged out the stepladder and climbed up to the top shelf. He pushed aside the sacks of sticky rice.

There was the bottle of golden delicious honey.

"I wonder if someone climbed up and drank the honey in the middle of the night. I must check."

And Kham took off the cap to check.

It looked like honey. It smelled like honey. But there was only one way to be certain.

Kham dipped his finger into the thick golden liquid and smeared it on his tongue.

"Yum! This is most definitely honey. But maybe only the top of the bottle is honey. Maybe there is a liquid beneath the honey that looks like honey but isn't. I must check."

"I'll try a little bit more just to make sure."

"I'll just take a few more drops."

And he took more drops and more drops and a few more drops.

"I'll just take a few more drops."

But there were no more drops.

Kham drummed the bottom of the bottle, but there was no more honey. Kham had drained the entire bottle.

"That was wonderful honey. Absolutely delicious."

"I think that I might have a problem," thought Kham as he licked his lips.

A few days later the abbot returned to the temple.

"Kham, get the ladder and bring me my honey."

Kham dragged out the ladder again and climbed up. He pushed aside the sacks of sticky rice. The bottle was much lighter now.

"Sir, something terrible has happened," said Kham as he brought down the much lighter bottle of honey. "The honey appears to be all gone!"

"How could that have happened?" asked the abbot.

"Flies. Look at the flies buzzing all around. And there is a fly on the bottle."

And, though monks are not supposed to get angry, the monk was furious with the flies that had stolen his honey. The monk was huffing and puffing, red-faced with anger.

"Flies! How I hate these creatures! Take a stick and kill them all!"

Kham grabbed a stick and chased the flies that buzzed around the room. He swung and whacked and whapped his stick, missing most but smashing a few.

A fly landed right on the abbot's nose. This did not escape Kham's notice.

"Sir, should I kill all the flies?" asked Kham, staring at the fly dancing on the abbot's nose.

"Every last one of them," said the abbot

"Every one?"

"Yes!"

Kham looked at the fly on the abbot's nose and smiled.

"Whatever you say." He took the stick and smacked the fly on the abbot's nose.

"Owww!" shrieked the abbot as he rubbed the dead fly from his very red nose.

"I got that one," said Kham with a satisfied smile.

MONKEY HEARTS FOR LUNCH

A long winding river wound its way through a beautiful forest filled with trees. The rivers were dotted with islands covered with lush vegetation. Two crocodiles lived in the river, a mother crocodile and her son.

"I am hungry. I am so very very hungry," said the mother crocodile to her son. "I want to eat a monkey's heart."

"Yes. A monkey heart. That is just what I want to eat, too."

"A delicious dinner of fresh monkey hearts," said the mother crocodile. "That would be just right. But I don't see any monkeys."

Whooomp! A coconut fell to the ground from a nearby tree. There was a monkey scrambling up its trunk.

"Mother," whispered the son, "there is a monkey in the tree. A delicious monkey in the tree with a delicious monkey heart."

"But how will we catch the monkey?"

"I have an idea."

"Mr. Monkey! Mr. Monkey!" called the crocodile son as he swam in the river.

"Hello, Mr. Crocodile. What are you doing here?" asked the monkey as he scampered up to the top of the tree.

"I am just swimming around in the river. We crocodiles love to swim. Yesterday I swam over to that island in the middle of the river. On that island are the biggest, ripest, sweetest bananas in all the land. Big, beautiful yellow bananas. We crocodiles don't eat bananas. Do monkeys like bananas?"

"I love bananas. Bananas are my favorite food. But how can I get to the island? I cannot swim."

"That is no problem. You can sit on my back and I will take you there myself. I am not doing anything today. Just swimming around the river. Let's go to the island of the big beautiful bananas."

"That's very kind of you. I would love to go," said the monkey.

The monkey scrambled down the coconut tree and jumped on to the back of the crocodile.

"Now hold tight," said the crocodile. The crocodile swam away from the bank of the river and swam lazily down the river towards the island.

"This is quite nice," thought the monkey.

But then the crocodile dove deep into the river. The monkey held tight to the crocodile. He could not breathe. He could not swim.

The crocodile slapped his tail and swam back up to the surface. The monkey sputtered and spat and coughed. "Mr. Crocodile, I cannot swim. Why did you dive into the river?"

"Because, Mr. Monkey, I am going to eat your tasty monkey heart. Monkey hearts are our favorite food. They are delicious!"

"Do you want to eat my heart? Why didn't you tell me? I left my heart up in the coconut tree."

"You don't have your heart with you?"

"No. I didn't want it to get wet. My heart is safe up there. If you want my heart, take me back to the bank of the river and I will give you my heart."

So the crocodile slapped his mighty tail and swam back to the land. The monkey jumped off the back of the crocodile and scrambled up the coconut tree.

"Ah, my heart is here. Right where I left it. Come on up, Mr. Crocodile, I have my tasty monkey heart ready for you to eat. Climb on up."

"Mr. Monkey, you know that crocodiles cannot climb trees."

"Of course, I forgot. I can solve that problem. I will tie a rope around you and we will lift you up."

"Fine. That will work."

The monkey jumped down the tree and took a long rope and tied it under the crocodile's front legs.

"Are you ready, Mr. Crocodile?"

"Ready, let's go. I am getting hungry for a monkey heart."

The monkey called all of his monkey friends to help pull the rope. They all pulled and yanked and pulled and yanked until the crocodile was dangling half way up the tree.

"Pull me up, monkeys. Pull me up. I can't reach the monkey heart from here. Pull me up."

But the monkeys just sat in the branches of the trees holding the rope and laughing and laughing and laughing.

"No, Mr. Crocodile, we will not pull you up. You will stay just like that, hanging in the air."

The crocodile looked up and saw the top the coconut tree and looked down at the group of monkeys holding the rope, laughing at him.

"I want to go back down. Let me down. Let me down now!"

"We will let you down if you promise never to eat monkey hearts again."

"But monkey hearts are my favorite food."

"Fine. No problem. Stay swinging in our coconut tree for weeks, months, years. We don't care."

"No, no, wait, please. Okay, I promise that I will never eat monkey hearts ever again."

"Down you go."

And all the monkeys let go of the rope at once. The crocodile landed on the ground with a big thwomp!

He dove into the river and swam away as fast he could to join his mother.

"Where are the monkey hearts?" asked his mother.

"Mother, I don't really like monkey hearts. Let's eat some mouse tails or frog fingers instead."

HOW XIENG MIENG
GOT HIS NAME

One day Kham was bathing in the river. A group of merchants were resting on the bank of the river. They were carrying big baskets of *mieng*. *Mieng* is a tea leaf that is used to wrap a popular Lao snack. Kham loved to snack on *mieng*.

"Novice," called the merchant to Kham. "How deep is this river? Where is the best place to cross it?"

"I think you cannot cross the river," said Kham.

"Of course I can cross the river," said the merchant. "I've crossed this river many times before. The water is just above your waist."

"If you are certain that you can cross the river then let's make a bet. If you can cross the river, I will give you all of my clothes. If you cannot cross the river, then you must give me all of your *mieng*."

"Ha ha!" scoffed the merchant. "We take your bet. Prepare to give us your clothes."

The merchants picked up their baskets of *mieng*, took off their sandals, hiked up their trousers, and headed into the river.

"This is easy. This river is not deep at all."

The merchants crossed to the other bank, rolled down their trousers and put their sandals back on.

"So, novice, we crossed the river. We have won the bet. Now hand us your clothes."

"You did not cross the river. You did not win the bet. You only walked through the river. To cross the river means that you must jump from one bank to the other. This you did not do. You have lost the bet. Now please hand me the *mieng*."

"We crossed the river. Now hand over your clothes."

"You did not cross the river. Hand over your *mieng*."

And Kham and the merchants argued and argued and argued.

"Let's take this case to the king," said Kham.

"An excellent idea," said the merchant. "Let's let the king decide."

So Kham and the merchants, with their baskets filled with *mieng*, walked to the king's palace.

The king welcomed the merchants and Kham. He listened to both sides of the argument over cups of tea.

The king considered the arguments.

"Merchants of *mieng*, Kham, I have come to a decision. Kham, you are half right and merchants, you are half right. Therefore, merchants, you do not need to give Kham all of your *mieng*. But you must give him four baskets and five bowls of *mieng*.

"You are a king of great wisdom," said Kham. "That is a wise decision. Now, dear merchants, if you will kindly wait for a few minutes I will return with four baskets and five alms bowls."

A few hours later the king and the merchants watched sixteen of the kingdom's strongest men carry four of the kingdom's largest baskets into the palace grounds.

"Where is Kham?" asked the king.

"Here I am, Your Majesty," said a voice inside a basket.

And Kham jumped out of the basket holding five alms bowls.

"You tricked us again!" complained the merchants.

"I did no such thing," said Kham. "The king said fill four baskets and five alms bowls. Are these not baskets? Are these not alms bowls?"

And Kham and the sixteen strong men laughed and laughed as they filled the huge baskets with the merchants' *mieng*.

"Kham," said the king, "as you know, it is against the law of the temple for novices to bet. Therefore I must ask you to leave your life as a novice."

And that is how Xieng Mieng got his name. Xieng is the title for a person who was once a novice. And Mieng is the word for tea leaves.

THE TUG OF WAR

One day a clever rabbit was hopping through the jungle. He spied a big elephant munching sugar cane stalks.

"Uncle Elephant!" called the rabbit. "Uncle Elephant!"

The elephant's ears were big, but he was not able to hear the small voice of the small rabbit.

"UNCLE ELEPHANT!" screamed the rabbit.

"Who is calling me?" asked the elephant flapping his mighty ears.

"I am! Down here, Uncle Elephant."

"Oh, hello little rabbit. What do you want?" The elephant lowered his head to hear the rabbit.

"Uncle Elephant, can I tie a rope around your foot?"

"Now why would you want to tie a rope around my foot?" asked the elephant.

"I challenge you to a tug-a-war, Uncle Elephant. I am going to drag you into the river."

"Ha! You, a tiny rabbit, are going to drag me, a huge elephant, into that river? Ha!" scoffed the elephant.

"So then you are not afraid?"

"Ha ha! Me? Afraid of a teeny tiny rabbit? Okay, I will play your game. Go ahead and tie a rope around my foot."

And that is exactly what the rabbit did.

"Now, Uncle Elephant, don't tug on the rope until I tug first."

"Sure," laughed the elephant, "but are you sure that I will feel your tug. Ha ha!"

And the elephant laughed and laughed, picked up another stalk of sugar cane and returned to munching his favorite snack.

The rabbit hopped down to the bank of the Mekong River. He slapped the river with his paws.

"Uncle Catfish!" he cried. "Uncle Catfish!"

But the rabbit saw no catfish in the flowing river.

The rabbit picked up the biggest rock that he could lift and threw it into the river.

"Uncle Catfish!" he cried, "Uncle Catfish!"

But still the catfish did not appear.

The rabbit then found a big boulder on the riverbank. He pushed and he shoved and finally loosened the boulder from the earth. He pushed and shoved and pushed and shoved and, finally, rolled the boulder into the river with big KERSPLASH!

"UNCLE CATFISH!" called the rabbit. "Uncle Catfish!"

The surface of the river was broken by a giant fish. It was a pla buek, the giant Mekong catfish.

"Who is rolling boulders into my river?" demanded the catfish.

"I am sorry, Uncle Catfish. I just wanted to get your attention."

"Oh, hello little rabbit. What do you want?" The catfish swam close to the shore to hear the voice of the rabbit.

"Uncle Catfish, can I tie a rope around your tail?"

"Now why would you want to tie a rope around my tail?"

"I challenge you to a tug-a-war, Uncle Catfish. I am going to drag you onto the shore."

"Ha! You, a tiny rabbit, are going to drag me, a huge catfish, onto the shore? Ha!" scoffed the catfish.

"So then you are not afraid?"

"Ha! Me? Afraid of a teeny tiny rabbit? Okay, I will play your game. Go ahead and tie a rope around my tail."

And that is exactly what the rabbit did.

"When I yell tug, you tug the rope as hard as you can and try to drag me into the river. Don't laugh. I am much stronger than you think."

And the rabbit hopped along the rope into the forest. When he was safely behind a bush he yelled, "Tug!"

"Whap!" The catfish slapped his mighty tail.

"Waaaaah!" yelled the elephant when he felt the rope tug on his leg. "That little rabbit is very strong." And the elephant yanked the rope.

"Waaaah!" yelled the catfish. "That tiny rabbit is quite strong." And the catfish yanked the rope.

"Yah!" yelled the elephant and tugged the rope.

"Yee!" yelled the catfish and tugged the rope.

The elephant was pulled slowly towards the river. The catfish was pulled slowly to the shore.

"I cannot believe that a teeny tiny rabbit can be so strong," thought the catfish. And the catfish looked onto the shore and saw the rope. But the rope was not tied to the rabbit but to his friend, the elephant.

"How can a little itsy-bitsy rabbit have such strength," thought the elephant. And the elephant looked at the rope and saw that it curled through the forest and into the river. "Can the rabbit swim too?" But then he saw his old friend, the catfish.

The elephant stomped his foot with anger and the earth shook. The catfish slapped his huge tail causing waves to crash on the riverbank.

"I'll get you, little rabbit. I will grab you with my trunk and toss you into the river."

"And when I catch you I will slap you with my tail back to the elephant."

"We will have a game of *kataw* and you will be the *kataw*."

And the elephant stomped through the jungle searching for the tricky rabbit.

"Where are you, little rabbit? Mr. Catfish and I are going to play a little game of *kataw*."

Where was the rabbit? He was hiding inside the skull of a dead horse.

"Where is that silly rabbit?" said the elephant, searching through the high grass.

From the floor of the jungle, from the skull of a dead horse, the elephant heard a small voice.

"Elephant, do not look for the rabbit. The body of the rabbit is small, but the strength of the rabbit is great."

"Who is that talking?"

"Look down," said the voice from the skull. "Look down at the jungle floor. It is me, the dead horse. Listen, elephant, I was alive. Alive as you are now. But I made a big mistake. I laughed at the rabbit. The rabbit pointed his paw at me. The next thing I knew I was dead."

"The little rabbit killed you? I don't believe it."

"Believe it. Now you are big and strong. You stomp your foot and the earth shakes. But I was big and strong like you. Look at me now. I am dead. Now, listen and take my advice. Go back and don't ever bother the rabbit again."

The elephant stared at the skull of the horse.

"The rabbit killed you?"

"Yes. Now stop thinking and go."

The elephant walked to the bank of the river.

"Brother Catfish, beware the rabbit. It has deadly magical powers. Beware."

The enormous elephant turned around and slowly walking away. The floor of the jungle shook with each step. The catfish slapped his tail and dove deep into the river. Waves crashed on the banks of the Mekong. And the little rabbit hopped out of the skull and away into the jungle.

WHAT'S IN THE BAMBOO TUBE?

In the kingdom there lived a very successful merchant named Xieng Nyan. Xieng Nyan thought he was very clever. He thought that he was the cleverest man in the kingdom.

One day a customer walked into his shop. There was a beautiful red rose on the counter.

"Isn't my rose beautiful?" Xieng Nyan asked. "It's from my own garden. It also has a wonderful fragrance. Please smell it."

The customer sniffed the rose.

Splurt! A stream of water splashed the customer's face.

It was a squirting flower!

"Ha ha ha!" laughed Xieng Nyan. "I tricked you!"

"You did," said the customer. "You are very clever."

"Who is the cleverest man in the kingdom?"

"Xieng Nyan you are indeed very clever but the cleverest man in the kingdom is Xieng Mieng."

A few days later, Latsamy, an old friend of Xieng Nyan strolled into his shop.

"Hello, my friend," said Xieng Nyan with a warm smile. "I want to show you something that just came into the shop. This is a looking glass. Put it up to your eye. Things far away look close. Here, try it."

Latsamy eagerly took the looking glass and pressed it to his eye. He looked towards the hills. He could see the individual trees that made up the forest.

"Thank you very much," said Latsamy, handing back the looking glass.

Xieng Nyan looked at Latsamy's face and could barely control his laughter.

"By the way, Latsamy, did you get into a fight?"

"Huh? Why do you say that?"

Xieng Nyan held up a mirror so that Latsamy could see the dark black circle around his eye.

"Ha ha ha!" laughed Xieng Nyan. "I tricked you, Latsamy."

"Yes you did," said Latsamy. "That was a very clever trick."

"So, Latsamy, who do you think is the cleverest man in this kingdom?"

"If I may be quite frank, the cleverest man in this kingdom is Xieng Mieng."

The next day, Sivath was walking past Xieng Nyan's house.

"Sivath, my good friend, please come in. My wife has just made some papaya salad. Come in and have some."

"Thank you. Don't mind if I do."

"Sivath, let me get you some soap and water. Always remember to wash your hands before every meal."

Xieng Nyan brought out a fresh cake of soap. He poured water over Sivath's hands as he lathered up.

"Yikes!" yelled Sivath, "my hands are turning black!"

"I tricked you," said Xieng Nyan.

"You did," said Sivath. "You are very clever."

"Who is the cleverest man in the kingdom?"

"Xieng Mieng, everyone knows that," replied Sivath.

"Xieng Mieng, Xieng Mieng, Xieng Mieng! All I ever hear is how clever this Xieng Mieng is. I will find this Xieng Mieng and then I will trick him. Then everyone will know that I, Xieng Nyan, am the cleverest man in the kingdom. But now I must come up with a really clever trick."

Xieng Nyan thought and thought and thought.

And then one afternoon, after a particularly satisfying lunch, it came to him.

"Aha! I know how I shall trick this Xieng Mieng. Now we will see who is the cleverest man in this kingdom."

And this is what he did: He ate an entire bowl of boiled peanuts.

"Peanuts cause gas," cautioned Xieng Nyan's wife.

Xieng Nyan took a bamboo tube down from the shelf.

Then he farted into the tube and quickly covered it tightly.

"Hee hee," he laughed to himself and set out for Xieng Mieng's village.

Xieng Mieng's village was far away. Xieng Nyan had to cross seven rivers to get to Xieng Mieng's village.

When he had finally crossed the seventh river, Xieng Nyan was very hot and very tired and very thirsty.

A man walked up to Xieng Nyan and said: "Greetings, welcome to our village. You must have come from a great distance. Please join me for a cup of coffee."

"Thank you very much," said Xieng Nyan. "That is very kind of you."

Xieng Nyan and his kind host sat down and drank cups of delicious Lao coffee.

"Now what good breeze has brought you to our village?" asked the man with a smile.

"I've come here to meet Xieng Mieng."

"Is that so? What business do you have with him?"

"I am a merchant from a village seven rivers crossing from here. I am a very clever merchant. But people have said that Xieng Mieng is more clever than me. I have come to trick Xieng Mieng."

"How?" asked the man.

"Do you see this bamboo tube? I am going to use it to trick Xieng Mieng. I am going to open its cover and have Xieng Mieng smell the tube. Guess what is inside."

"I wouldn't know," said the man.

"My fart!" laughed Xieng Nyan.

"You farted in the bamboo tube?" laughed the man. "You are indeed a clever man. But I just had a thought. When did you fart in the bamboo tube?"

"When I was back at my house in my village," answered Xieng Nyan.

"That was such a long time ago. Are you sure that your fart will still smell? Maybe your fart lost it smell."

"I don't think so," said Xieng Nyan.

"I would not take a chance. Think how foolish you would look if you asked Xieng Mieng to smell your fart and there was no fart. You should smell it."

"You have a point," said Xieng Nyan.

Xieng Nyan opened the bamboo tube. When he smelled it his face suddenly changed. "Yes, the fart is definitely still there."

"Ha ha ha!" laughed the other man. "Do you know who I am? I am Xieng Mieng. I am more clever than you."

Xieng Nyan walked back to his village knowing that Xieng Mieng was, indeed, the cleverest man in the kingdom.

THE MAGIC CLOTH CONTEST

Xieng Nyan returned to his village. He had lost a lot of face when Xieng Mieng tricked him into smelling his own fart. He spent days and days trying to concoct a way to trick Xieng Mieng.

One day a traveling merchant came to Xieng Nyan's village. Xieng Nyan was very excited by a piece of merchandise that the man had for sale. Xieng Nyan happily purchased this remarkable piece. "Ha!" Xieng Nyan shouted. "Now I can defeat Xieng Mieng."

The next day Xieng Nyan walked to Xieng Mieng's village.

"Xieng Mieng," said Xieng Nyan, "I challenge you to a contest."

"What kind of contest would that be?" asked Xieng Mieng.

"A magic cloth contest. I will bring a cloth and you bring a cloth. The judge will decide whose cloth is more magical. But, Xieng Mieng, I warn you that I have the most amazing cloth in the land."

"A magic cloth contest? How interesting! Of course I accept. I think that the judge will find that I have the most amazing cloth in the land," said Xieng Mieng.

But the truth was that Xieng Mieng had no magic cloth.

Xieng Mieng had two shirts, two pairs of trousers, and a *pa salong*, an old tattered blue cloth he used for bathing But he had no magic cloth.

But Xieng Mieng had a clever mind and he laughed when he conceived his plan.

The day of the contest arrived. Many people came from far and wide.

Xieng Nyan smiled as he displayed an exquisite lacquer box decorated with precious jewels. Xieng Mieng brought a humble woven sticky rice basket.

"Xieng Nyan, would you be kind enough to show us your magic cloth?" asked the judge.

"Certainly," said Xieng Nyan. "I am pleased to show you my magic cloth."

Xieng Nyan slowly opened his box and carefully pulled out a dazzling gold silk scarf of intricate design.

"It is a lovely piece of cloth, Xieng Nyan," said Xieng Mieng. "But I see no magic."

"Be patient, Xieng Mieng, the magic will soon be revealed. Prepare to be amazed!"

Xieng Nyan raised the cloth above of head and—phwoop!—gave it a shake.

Small puffs of smoke rose to the sky.

He shook it again. And more smoke billowed from the cloth.

"Ooh! Aah!" gasped the audience.

"Amazing!" whispered an awed spectator. "Smoke from a cloth, yet there is no fire."

The crowd cheered.

Xieng Nyan offered a *wai* and bowed to the audience, folded the cloth, and put it back into the box.

"A cloth that smokes?" said Xieng Mieng. "What magic is there in that? Don't you realize that smoking causes cancer? I suggest you take that cloth to the doctor for a checkup."

The audience snickered.

"Now, judges, Xieng Nyan, ladies and gentlemen, you will see real magic!"

Xieng Mieng pulled the top off the sticky rice basket. He blew on his hands as he rubbed them together. Then he lowered his hands in the basket and raised them above his head.

"Ladies and gentlemen, as you can clearly see with your own eyes, I am holding above my head a cloth woven from invisible thread!"

He displayed the cloth to his left and to his right so that all could easily see.

The audience gasped. The audience cheered.

"Amazing! Xieng Mieng is holding a cloth but you cannot see it. It is an invisible cloth!"

"Hah!" sneered Xieng Nyan. "What nonsense. I don't believe it. I don't see any cloth made from invisible thread."

"Of course not, you fool," retorted Xieng Mieng. "The thread is invisible and, of course, the cloth is invisible. If you can see the cloth then it is not invisible. Can't you understand that?"

"That's ridiculous," snapped Xieng Nyan.

"It's magic," replied Xieng Mieng. "Let's hear from the judges."

The judges excused themselves and walked over to the coffee shop. After enjoying their cups of coffee they returned.

"We have reached our decision," said the oldest of the judges. "Xieng Nyan's smoking cloth and Xieng Mieng's invisible cloth are both quite magical. We declare it a tie."

"Harrumph!" snorted Xieng Nyan. "That invisible cloth is sheer tomfoolery. How could anyone believe that?"

"Harrumph!" snorted Xieng Mieng. "How could a smoking cloth compare to the magic of an invisible cloth? This is an outrage."

Xieng Mieng picked up his box and walked back to his house grumbling to himself: "How could the judges not have realized the magic of this invisible cloth? It is obvious to anyone that a smoking cloth is a mere trick."

Xieng Mieng walked back into his house, put the sticky rice basket back on a shelf in the kitchen, and laughed and laughed and laughed.

THE BIRD THAT SPOKE FIVE
LANGUAGES FLUENTLY

Xieng Nyan was very upset. He had been certain that his golden smoking cloth would win the magic cloth contest. But he had had to return to his village in defeat. He had lost face again.

Now he was even more determined to defeat Xieng Mieng.

But how?

A few weeks passed. A merchant from a land to the north came to Xieng Nyan's village. He had many wondrous items for sale, but what caught Xieng Nyan's attention was a talented mynah bird in a golden cage.

"Xieng Nyan, this handsome bird is the most amazing bird I have ever seen. It can speak five languages fluently. This little bird can speak Lao, Vietnamese, Chinese, English, and French. And it can speak these languages with a lovely sweet voice—a voice sweeter than the *apsaras* in heaven. But don't take my word for it. Let's listen to the bird."

And the man took the bird out of the cage. The mynah really did speak five languages. And the mynah really did have a lovely sweet soft voice.

"I'll take it," said Xieng Nyan and pulled gold coins from his pouch picturing in his mind how he would use this talented bird to defeat Xieng Mieng.

"Xieng Mieng, I challenge you to another contest," said Xieng Nyan.

"Of course; what kind of contest do you propose?"

"A talking bird contest," said Xieng Nyan with a smile.

"How interesting," said Xieng Mieng. "And what exactly are the rules of the contest?"

"The winner of the contest will be the person who displays the bird that can speak the most languages and can speak the most sweetly."

"I accept," said Xieng Mieng.

Xieng Mieng had no talking bird. But Xieng Mieng had a plan.

The next morning Xieng Mieng trekked into the forest with the body of a dead chicken and a net. He placed the chicken on the net and set it on the ground. Then he waited in the shade of a tall tree.

Soon a big brown vulture swooped down to peck at the carcass of the dead chicken.

"Squawk!" cried the vulture.

Xieng Mieng yanked a cord that closed the net. He had captured the vulture.

"Squawk!" cried the vulture.

Xieng Mieng carried the squawking vulture in the net to his house and put it in a big cage.

The next day he bought some mynah birds from the village market.

"Squawk!" cried the vulture. It was hungry.

Xieng Mieng tossed the mynah bird into the vulture's cage. The vulture gobbled it down.

Everyday Xieng Mieng gave the vulture one mynah bird for its daily meal.

The day of the contest arrived. Again people came from miles around to witness the contest. Xieng Nyan brought a beautiful gold cage covered with an expensive silk cloth. Xieng Mieng brought a simple bamboo cage covered with his *pa salong*.

"I can see that your invisible cloth is visible today," snorted Xieng Nyan.

"Aren't you concerned that the smoking cloth with choke your bird?" asked Xieng Mieng.

"Gentlemen," said the judge, "this is not the magic cloth contest. This is the talking bird contest. Now shall we begin? Let us see your birds."

With a flourish Xieng Nyan lifted the cloth.

"Good afternoon, ladies and gentlemen," said the mynah bird.

Xieng Mieng removed the *pa salong* from the cage.

"Squawk!" said the vulture.

"My bird will go first, if you don't mind."

Xieng Nyan took his mynah bird from his cage.

"Thank you very much for inviting me to the talking bird contest," said the mynah bird.

"This mynah also speaks French," said Xieng Nyan.

"Bonjour, la plume de ma tante est sur le bureau de mon oncle."

"And Vietnamese."

"Làm ơn đừng hút thuốc."

"And Chinese."

"针灸疼不疼？"

"And Lao."

"ສະບາຍດີບໍ່"

"Wonderful! Bravo! Fantastic!" cheered the audience. They had never heard a bird that could speak five languages.

"I am honored to speak to your species, *homo sapiens*, on the topic 'The Mynah Bird: Sacred Bird of Ancient India.' The mynah was considered sacred by the Indian people and on feast days the mynah bird was pulled through the city on oxen . . . "

The audience stood open mouthed as the bird lectured away in English.

"That's an amazing bird but what is it saying?"

"I don't know. I only speak Lao."

While everyone was listening to the lecture of the mynah bird, Xieng Mieng opened his cage.

Out hopped the vulture.

"Squawk!" squawked the vulture, interrupting the lecture.

The vulture hopped on to the stage, right next to the mynah bird.

"Squawk!"

The vulture opened his huge beak and gobbled down the mynah bird.

"What have you done?" yelled Xieng Nyan. "What have you done? Your ugly brown vulture has eaten my mynah bird. You have lost this contest and now you must pay me back for my mynah bird."

"I have not lost this contest. I will not pay for your bird. And shame on you for training a mynah bird to speak such vulgar foul words! Don't you remember the rules of the contest? The bird must speak sweetly. Your mynah bird used crude nasty words in five different languages. My beautiful vulture understood the mynah's lecture. He was furious. Such dirty words. Such vulgar language! Of course he was angry. And so he ate the mynah bird."

"My mynah bird did not use bad language," protested Xieng Nyan.

Xieng Mieng and Xieng Nyan argued and argued and argued.

"Gentlemen, gentlemen," said the judge, "please settle down. We would like to discuss this case and determine who won this contest."

The judges huddled in a circle. They spoke calmly as they considered the contestants.

"Xieng Mieng, Xieng Nyan, we have come to a decision. It is a tie."

"Squawk!" squawked the vulture.

"Come, my beautiful bird," said Xieng Mieng. "Let's go home. I am sorry that you had to hear such disgusting language. Are you still hungry?"

THE LION'S LUNCH

The lion took a deep breath and puffed out his powerful chest and let out an earth-shaking roar.

The animals trembled with fear. They scurried deep into the forest, climbed up high into the trees and plunged deep into the river.

"That was fun," smiled the lion with satisfaction.

"Animals, I am finished roaring. You can come back out of the jungle. You can come down from the trees. You can come out of the rivers. I have had my dinner. We can play now. We can have some fun together."

But, of course, none of the animals came out of the jungle, or down from the trees, or out of the rivers. No animals wanted to play with the lion.

The lion was not happy. Something was missing in his life.

Friends. The lion had no friends. He had no one to play with.

The next week the lion called a meeting of all of the animals in the jungle. They all came—the monkeys, the frogs, the toads, the snakes, the crocodiles, the bears, the deer, the birds, and the rabbits all came.

"Welcome, animals. Thank you very much for coming to this meeting. I have called you here to discuss something very important to me. But first, I have a question: Who is the king of the jungle?"

"This is easy," said the wolf. "You, great lion. You are the king of the jungle."

"And why am I the king of the jungle?" asked the lion.

"Because, you are the strongest and you are the fastest, and you eat us," he answered.

"Absolutely correct. Ten points. Of course I eat you. I am an animal. You are animals. You eat every day and I eat every day. The difference is that I eat you and you don't eat me. But we lions have feelings too. We like to play and laugh and talk. I have a problem. I have no friends. Will you be my friend?"

The animals were silent.

"I know that you are afraid of me but I have a plan whereby we can all live together peacefully. We can play together and enjoy our lives. Here is the plan: Every day one animal will come to my den at lunchtime. I will eat that animal. You make a schedule and decide which animal will be my lunch. Then we can be friends. We can be friends before I eat you. Will you agree to that?"

The animals talked and yelled and screamed and argued. It was difficult for the animals to come to a decision. But finally they agreed.

And the animals did live peacefully. But the animals did not live happily. Every day an animal would come to the lion's den to be the lion's lunch.

One day it was the rabbit's turn to be eaten.

"Hello, rabbit. Welcome to my den," said the lion smacking his lips at the sight of the fat little rabbit.

"Lion, before you eat me I have something to talk with you about," said the rabbit.

"Very well," said the lion.

"This morning I went down to the pond for my last bath. I wanted to be nice and clean before you ate me. In the pond I saw a big lion. The lion said that he wanted to eat me. I told him that he could not eat me because I was going to be your lunch today."

"What?" roared the lion. "There is another lion in my forest who wants to eat my food? Where is this lion?"

"I will take you to see him. But please don't let him eat me. I want you to eat me. After all, you are our king."

And the rabbit led the lion on a walk through the forest, the rabbit hopping ahead of it.

"Where is this lion?"

"Just a bit further. Through those trees and on the top of that cliff. You can look down from the cliff to the pond. You can see the lion from there."

The lion ran ahead of the rabbit and bounded up the cliff.

And from the top of the cliff he looked into the pond.

And, sure enough, he saw a lion in the pond.

"How dare you come into my forest? How dare you try to eat my food?" roared the lion. The lion in the pool opened his mouth to roar too but no sound came from his mouth.

"What do you have to say for yourself?" roared the lion.

The other lion just opened his mouth but no there was no sound.

"You dare to mock me, lion? I'll show you who is the king of this jungle!"

The lion leaped into the pond.

Unfortunately for the lion, the pond was shallow and filled with sharp rocks.

The lion hit his head on a rock.

And so the rabbit did not become the lion's lunch. In fact, the lion never ate lunch again.

And the clever rabbit and the animals of that jungle played and laughed and sang and lived peacefully ever after.

XIENG MIENG'S REVENGE

The king had been following the contests of Xieng Mieng and Xieng Nyan. He was amused by Xieng Mieng's trickery and pleased that someone else had been the victim of Xieng Mieng's clever mind.

"So, Xieng Mieng," said the king with a chuckle. "I have heard how you defeated Xieng Nyan. You are, indeed, a very clever man."

"I am flattered that you say that, Your Majesty, but I am just a simple man. I know that you are far cleverer than me."

"It is not easy to trick such a clever man," said the king. "I have invited you to the palace for a special dinner to celebrate your triumph. I have asked the royal cooks to prepare a special curry in your honor."

"That is very kind, Your Majesty."

The king clapped his hand. The king's servants brought a large tray filled with dishes kept warm beneath silver lids. The servants uncovered the dishes and scooped the food onto Xieng Mieng's plate. But the king's plate was empty.

"Your Majesty, you are not joining me in this meal?"

"As much as I would like to, I will not be able to join you for dinner. Unfortunately, I have been called unexpectedly to confer with an ambassador from a neighboring kingdom. But I do hope that you enjoy your special meal. Please come back tomorrow morning and tell me how you enjoyed it."

The king left the room. Xieng Mieng tucked into his aromatic curry.

The next morning Xieng Mieng returned to the king's palace.

"So, Xieng Mieng, how did you enjoy last night's meal?"

"It was truly delicious. Thank you for inviting me."

"It was a new recipe that our cooks created. Did you recognize the ingredients?"

"Certainly, there was a lot of chili and pepper and lemon grass and coconut milk."

"Indeed, but what about the meat?"

"Chicken."

"Close."

"Duck?"

"Not exactly. Guess again."

"Guinea fowl? Could it have been guinea fowl?"

"I'm sorry, Xieng Mieng. You are wrong again. Would you like to know what kind of bird it was?"

"Yes."

"Vulture," laughed the king. "We cooked up your vulture. I tricked you Xieng Mieng!"

A few weeks later Xieng Mieng and other citizens of the kingdom were invited to the palace to discuss plans for civic improvement. There was a big blackboard in the front of the room.

"Next to the market we will plant some teak trees."

The king picked up a piece of chalk to draw on the blackboard.

But, for some reason, the chalk would not write.

"Lick the chalk, Your Majesty," suggested Xieng Mieng, "then the chalk will write."

The king licked the chalk. He tried writing on the blackboard but it still did not write.

"Lick it again, Your Majesty," said Xieng Mieng.

The king licked the chalk again and tried to write on the blackboard but still it would not write.

Xieng Mieng picked up the piece of chalk and examined it closely.

"Oh, Your Majesty, there has been a terrible mistake. This is not chalk. This is a vulture dropping. Your Majesty, how did it taste?"

SPEED VS. CUNNING

One day a rabbit was sitting at the edge of a pond. The rabbit was watching a snail slide by. The rabbit chuckled with laughter at the snail.

"Mr. Snail," laughed the rabbit. You sure do walk funny."

"Oh, Mr. Rabbit, why do you say that?" asked the snail.

"Because, my dear snail, you walk so slowly and leave a trail of slime."

"I walk the way I walk. You walk the way you walk. I don't laugh at the way you walk. Why do you laugh at the way I walk? That is not polite. What is wrong with walking slowly and leaving a lovely trail of shimmering slime? Let's continue this discussion in the shade. I'll meet you under that tree."

The rabbit hopped through the tall grass over to the tree. He snacked on some tender leaves of grass. And then he lay down for a nap.

A few hours later the snail arrived.

"So, Mr. Snail, you are here at last. What took you so long?"

"Why speed? I want to smell the flowers, listen to the birds, watch the changing sky. I want to draw a beautiful figure 8 in shiny slime. What is the point of going fast? But I can go fast if that is what I want to do. In fact, I can go faster, much faster than you."

"Faster than me? Ha! Every animal knows that a rabbit is much, much faster than a snail."

"Clearly, those animals have a lot to learn. I challenge you to a race. Same time, same place, tomorrow."

"Are you serious? Okay, I'll see you here tomorrow. Oh, Mr. Snail, don't forget to put on your running shoes. Ha ha ha!"

The rabbit hopped home and told the other rabbits about the snail. The rabbits laughed and laughed. Then Mr. Rabbit went to sleep with a big smile on his face, dreaming of the snail and his shiny trail.

But that evening, the snail called a meeting of his snail friends.

"My dear snails, the rabbit shows us no respect. He sneers at our snail trails, laughs at the way we walk. It is time that we taught him a lesson."

The snails hatched a clever plan.

Early the following morning the rabbit and the snail arrived at the bank of the pond.

"Are you ready for our race?" asked the snail.

"Of course. Are you ready to lose?" said the rabbit.

"You will see who will win this race. Here is the racecourse. We start here at the edge of the pond, then run through the tall grass once around the pond and finish right here. And may the fastest animal win. Are you ready? On your mark. Ready? Set. GO!"

The rabbit jumped up and bounded in giant rabbit hops around the pond. Soon he was at the halfway mark. He turned around to look at his opponent, but he saw no snail.

"Mr. Snail, where are you?" laughed the rabbit.

"Here I am," said a snail, but it was in front of him!

"Hurry up, Mr. Rabbit," said the snail in the tall grass. "See you at the finish line."

The rabbit could not believe it. How could a snail run faster than he? He jumped up and bounded in great rabbit hops. He hopped past the snail (who seemed hardly able to move at all) and hopped and hopped and hopped. He paused a moment to look back to see where the snail was.

"Mr. Snail, where are you?" said the rabbit, but he did not laugh this time.

"Here I am, Mr. Rabbit, right in front of you. Let's go."

The rabbit ran as fast as a rabbit could. "I cannot be beaten by a snail! What will the other animals say?"

But as he ran to the finish line he saw the snail.

"I won, Mr. Rabbit."

The rabbit did not know what to say.

"Who walks funny now, Mr. Rabbit?"

"Please, Mr. Snail, don't tell any animals about this race. I am sorry that I said that snails walk funny. I will never laugh at snails again."

And the rabbit turned around and hopped slowly away through the tall grass.

A few hours later, the snails all gathered at the finish line.

"Oh ho!" cheered the leader of the snails who started the race. "Snails united can beat a silly rabbit."

"That foolish ball of fur didn't even notice that my shell is shiny and yours is dull," said the snail that was stationed at the midway point.

"His shell may be dull, but his slime does shine!" said the snail that was at the finish line.

"Let's go slimin'!" shouted the snails.

And the snails sang a little snail song and laughed a little snail laugh and drew a shiny slimy figure 8 in the sand beside the pond.

The figure 8 took them three hours and twenty-seven minutes.

THE KING TRIES TO TRICK
XIENG MIENG

The weather in the kingdom was lovely. The sky was a bright blue and cool breezes played with the fluffy clouds.

"Xieng Mieng," said the king, "the weather is perfect for a picnic in the countryside. We will go to the pond near the forest."

"How will we get there?" asked Xieng Mieng, though he already knew the answer.

"I, being the king, will ride on my beautiful white horse and you, being Xieng Mieng, will walk."

"Of course, Your Majesty."

The king rode and Xieng Mieng walked out through the gates of the palace, through the rice fields and into the deep green forest to the bank of the pond.

The king and Xieng Mieng ate the picnic lunch prepared by the royal chefs. There was papaya salad and barbecued chicken and sticky rice. For dessert they ate mangoes. The horse ate some grass.

"Xieng Mieng," said the king, "you are a clever man. It is true that you have tricked me a few times. Now I challenge you to trick me again. I challenge you to trick me so that I will go into the pond. If you can trick me into going into the pond I will let you ride my horse back home."

"Your Majesty, you are much cleverer than I. You know that I cannot trick you into going into the pond."

"So, Xieng Mieng, then you admit that I am cleverer than you."

"Of course, Your Majesty, you are cleverer than me. But, Your Majesty, if you go into the pond, I can trick you into getting out of the pond."

"Hah! Let me see you try! I accept your challenge."

And the king walked into the pond.

"I am cleverer than you, Xieng Mieng," laughed the king as he stood in the middle of the pond.

Xieng Mieng sat down on the grass and finished up the rest of the mangoes.

"Xieng Mieng, here I am. I am in the pond. Now you try to trick me to come out of the pond."

Xieng Mieng yawned and lay down on the grass and took a nap.

"Xieng Mieng! I am in the pond! Now trick me into coming out of the pond!"

Xieng Mieng woke from his sleep. He yawned and stretched.

"It is getting late, Your Majesty. I must go back now. I cannot trick you to come out of the pond. Since you will be staying in the pond, you will not have any need for your horse. So I know it won't be a problem if I ride it back."

Xieng Mieng mounted the king's beautiful white horse.

"Wait! You tricked me again! Wait!" said the king as he watched a laughing Xieng Mieng go galloping away.

THREE FRIENDLY FLIES

Once upon a time there were three friendly flies. These three flies were the best of friends. Every day the three friendly flies would fly around here and fly around there. And every evening they would fly into their local coffee shop to taste a bit of this and taste a bit of that and talk about this and talk about that.

"I am bored flying around the same old place. Same old coffee shop. Same old coffee. Same old cups. Same old plates. Same old food," said one of the flies, whose name was Somboon.

"I agree," said another fly, whose name was Sombat. "We need to fly to a new place. Let's go somewhere new."

"I don't know," said the third fly, whose name was Somlat. "I like it here. This is our home."

"Let's go somewhere new, somewhere different," said Fly Somboon. "I have an idea. We are three flies, right?"

"Let me count," said Fly Somlat, who was learning to count. "One fly, two flies. No, I only count two flies."

"You forgot to count yourself," said Fly Somboon.

"Yes, of course, one fly, two flies, and me make three flies. You are right, Fly Somboon. We are three flies."

"Thank you, Fly Somlat," smiled Fly Somboon. "I have a plan. Tomorrow we will fly to three different houses. We will stay in each house for one week and then meet back here. We will have new things to talk about. We will have new experiences."

"We will have an adventure," said Fly Sombat.

"It will be exciting," said Fly Somlat.

"Excellent. Now I will assign you your new house. Somlat, you will go out into the countryside. You will be staying at the house of Farmer Bounmy."

"Okay," agreed Fly Somlat.

"Fly Sombat, you will be staying at the house of Merchant Bounma in the town."

"Very good," agreed Fly Sombat.

"And I will be staying at the palace of the king. Are we ready to fly? Agreed?"

"Agreed," said Fly Sombat and Fly Somlat.

And the three friendly flies ate a bit more of this and a bit more of that and talked a bit more about this and a bit more about that and said good-bye and flew away to their new homes.

One week later, the three friendly flies flew back to their local coffee shop.

"Hello, Fly Sombat. Hello, Fly Somlat," said Fly Somboon. Fly Somboon had a big smile on his fly face.

"You are looking very fat," said Fly Sombat. "Tell us about the king's palace."

"It was wonderful, fantastic. I have never seen so much food on one table. There was pork, beef, lamb, and duck. There were crabs, shrimp, and fish. And there was a whole platter of my favorite food, barbecued chicken!"

"Ooh!" exclaimed Fly Somlat and Fly Sombat, for barbecued chicken was the favorite food of the three friendly flies.

"I ate so much. I ate morning, noon, and night. Do you see how fat I am?"

Fly Somboon patted his newly round belly.

"Fly Sombat, tell us about your experience at the house of Merchant Bounma."

"I had a good time," said Fly Sombat. "There was plenty of food. We had a lot of chicken and pork. But when I landed on the food, he would throw it away. I am fit, but I am not fat."

Fly Somboon and Fly Somlat nodded with approval.

"How about you, Fly Somlat? Tell us about your life at Farmer Bounmy's house."

"Terrible. It was awful. Look at me. I am so thin. I didn't eat a thing."

"Tsk. Tsk. Tsk," sympathized Fly Sombat and Fly Somboon.

"Farmer Bounmy and his family ate everything at the table. When I landed on some food, they chased me away. I flew all over his house but I couldn't find any food. Now you see how thin I am."

"I am sorry, Fly Somlat," said Fly Somboon. "Here, have some coffee. I have a plan. Let's move to the king's palace. There is plenty of room and plenty of food. Let's pack our bags and fly there now. What do you say to that, dear fly friends?"

"Let's go! I am going to pack right now," said Fly Sombat.

"Don't forget to pack your toothbrush," advised Fly Somboon, because Fly Sombat did not brush after every meal.

"What about you Fly Somlat?" asked Fly Somboon.

"I don't know. I like it here."

"Please come," said Fly Sombat. "We are the three friendly flies. Without you we will be only two friendly flies. There will be a lot of food to eat. You will be fat like us."

"Please come," said Fly Somboon. "The king's palace won't be fun without you."

"Okay," agreed Fly Somlat at last. So the three friendly flies packed their bags (each with his own toothbrush) and flew out of the coffee shop, over the rice field, through the hills, and into the open window of the king's palace.

"Barbecued chicken! Lunch! Let's go!" said Fly Sombat.

The three friendly flies circled the table filled with heaping plates of hot tasty juicy barbecued chicken. Fly Somlat, the hungriest, dove for the drumstick. Fly Sombat went for the wing and Fly Somboon went for the breast.

But the flies were not alone.

Behind the curtains was a royal guard. And the royal guard was armed with the royal flyswatter.

Whap! The flyswatter landed smack on the drumstick but missed Fly Somlat by just a cat's whisker!

Whap! The flyswatter smacked a chicken wing but Fly Sombat saw it coming and scampered off the plate.

Whap! The flyswatter thumped the chicken breast but Fly Somboom had crawled underneath.

"Fly home! Fly home! Quick! Forget the chicken! Fly home!"

The three friendly flies flew from the table in a mad dash. The flyswatter slapped and smacked and whapped and thumped. The three flies felt the whoosh of the whack on their wings but they were skilled in evasive flying.

The three friendly flies flew through the window, out of the king's palace, over the rice fields, up and up and away.

That evening the three friendly flies flew in to their old coffee shop to eat a bit of this and taste a bit of that. They saw the same old cups. Same old plates. Same old food. Same old coffee."

"The coffee tastes very good today," said Fly Somboon.

A CURE FOR THE KING

It was not that long ago that people did not have television sets. They did not have the Internet, or cable TV, or satellite dishes or even radios. What did people do for entertainment in those days? They listened to stories. They would gather in the evening, after the work was done and tell stories. And if you were a king, you could listen to stories whenever you wanted to.

The king loved stories. He listened to stories morning, noon and night. He listened to stories while he was eating. He listened to stories while he was bathing. He even listened to stories while he was sleeping.

One morning, Mr. Somkhuanta came to see the king. He was met by the king's secretary.

"Excuse me," said Mr. Somkhuanta, "I have an urgent request. I would like to see the king as soon as possible."

"Certainly, Mr. Somkhuanta," said the king, because Mr. Somkhuanta was a well-respected citizen of the kingdom. "He will see you as soon as he has finished listening to a story."

"Thank you."

"Please wait here," said the secretary.

Mr. Somkhuanta waited. And he waited. And he waited. He waited the entire morning.

And he waited the entire afternoon.

And he waited the entire evening.

And he waited all through the night.

The next morning he was still waiting when the secretary came to work. "Excuse me, sir. I have an extremely urgent message for the king. I would like to see him as soon as possible. Is he finished listening to the story yet?"

"Let me just check. Please wait a moment."

After a few moments the secretary returned. "I am sorry, he is still listening to the story. Please wait a moment."

"Thank you."

But Somkhuanta waited the entire day. And he waited the next day. And the next day. And the next.

After a week, the secretary came from the king's office to find Somkhuanta snoozing on the floor. "Mr. Somkhuanta, the king has finished listening to his story. He will see you now."

Mr. Somkhuanta walked into the king's office.

"Mr. Somkhuanta, welcome. I have been listening to the most wonderful story. I do love listening to stories. Now, what is it that you would like to speak to me about."

"Your Majesty, I have the pleasure of personally inviting you to our village for our annual village festival."

"How wonderful," said the king. He clapped his hands in delight because Somkhuanta's village was famous for its festivals. "When will it be?"

"It was yesterday."

Then and there the king realized that he had a serious problem. He knew that he had to be cured of his habit of listening to stories.

"I know someone who can cure you of this habit," said the king's secretary.

"And who might that be?" asked the king.

"Why, Xieng Mieng, of course."

And so Xieng Mieng was summoned to the palace to cure the king of his addiction to stories.

"Your Majesty, I am going to tell you a wonderful tale that will cure your habit of listening to tales."

The king settled into his favorite chair and Xieng Mieng sat at his feet.

"Once upon a time there was a very big farm. The family of farmers grew corn. When the corn was harvested it was stored in a huge storehouse in back of the family's house. There was a hungry grasshopper that lived on the farm. The grasshopper loved to eat corn. The hungry grasshopper hopped, hopped, hopped to the storehouse and took a kernel of corn. Then the grasshopper hopped, hopped, hopped home and chewed and chewed and chewed the kernel of corn. Then the grasshopper hopped, hopped, hopped to the storehouse and took a kernel of corn. Then the grasshopper hopped, hopped, hopped home and chewed and chewed and chewed the kernel of corn. Then the grasshopper hopped, hopped, hopped to the storehouse and took a kernel of corn. Then the grasshopper hopped, hopped, hopped home and chewed and chewed and chewed the kernel of corn. Then the grasshopper hopped, hopped, hopped . . ."

The king squirmed in his chair, but Xieng Mieng repeated the same two sentences. Xieng Mieng repeated these same two sentences for hours and hours.

"Stop!" yelled the king. "Stop! I can't take it anymore. Stop the hopped, hopped, hopped and stop the chewed, chewed, chewed. Enough! No more stories!"

And that is how Xieng Mieng cured the king of his habit of listening to stories.

THE PAINTING CONTEST

One day a messenger arrived at the king's palace. He was from a peaceable kingdom seven rivers away.

"Your Majesty, our king wishes to invite an artist from your kingdom to compete in a painting contest. The winner of the prize will receive two gold necklaces."

"I would be honored to send our most outstanding artist."

"And what is name of your illustrious artist?"

"Hmmm, yes, hmmm," the king hummed and hawed because no name came to the royal mind. The kingdom really had no artists. When a mural needed to be painted, an artist was sent for.

"I will send a message to your king to tell him about the dietary and housing requirements of our illustrious artist."

"And who shall I say is coming?" asked the messenger.

"Ah . . . er . . . thank you very much. Please relay my warm regards to your king and I wish him health and longevity."

After the king dismissed the messenger, he called a meeting of his advisors. "We have been invited to send an artist to the annual painting contest. I have no idea who we should send. Do you have any suggestions?"

"I will go," said Xieng Mieng.

"You? You can't even draw a straight line."

"I will go. And I will win the contest."

The king had not seen any of Xieng Mieng's artistic talents but he knew that Xieng Mieng had other talents that would serve him well in the contest.

"Go, then, Xieng Mieng. And I wish you the best of luck."

The day of the contest arrived. Citizens from throughout the kingdom had gathered outside the palace wall to witness the contest.

"Welcome Xieng Mieng," said the king of the land several rivers away. "I am pleased that your king was able to send someone as illustrious as yourself to our humble contest. Let me introduce you to our artist. His name is Khamsone. He has painted the murals on my palace and our temples. I am certain that you will find him a worthy competitor."

"I am pleased to meet a fellow artist, Xieng Mieng. Tell me what your specialty is?"

"I paint walls white," laughed Xieng Mieng.

The artist was not amused. He was quite serious about his craft.

"Are we ready for the contest?" asked the king.

Both Xieng Mieng and the artist nodded.

"Please look at this palace wall. You both have a set of paints and brushes. You will have five minutes to draw an animal. Mr. Khamsone, you will go first. Mr. Xieng Mieng, you will follow. On your mark. Are you ready?"

"Ready," answered Mr. Khamsone.

"One, two, three, go!"

Artist Khamsone grabbed brushes in both of his hands and dipped them into bowls of paint. With dabs and strokes and flourishes of his talented hands he quickly created a striking picture of a peacock with magnificent feathers, perched on a tropical bush.

He bowed to the crowd as they cheered at the beautiful picture, which now graced the palace wall.

"Xieng Mieng, are you ready?"

"Ready."

"On you mark, one, two, three, go!"

Xieng Mieng sauntered to the wall. He dipped his hand into the bowl.

He dragged his fingers down the wall leaving five long brown streaks.

He turned around and bowed.

"Are you finished?" asked the judge.

"I am indeed."

"Ah, what is it?" asked the judge.

"Five of the noblest creatures on this planet. Earthworms, five earthworms. And it is clear that I have won this contest, thank you very much. For I have drawn five creatures while my worthy opponent has only drawn one."

"But, my peacock is a thing of beauty and your earthworms are, well, ugly."

"Mr. Khamsone, have you attended any classes in arithmetic. Is five not more than one? Judges, please decide."

The judges huddled for a few moments.

"Mr. Khamsone, we all agree that your painting if quite beautiful but Xieng Mieng did draw four more animals than you in the time allotted. Therefore, we pronounce Xieng Mieng the winner of the painting contest. We are happy to award you two gold necklaces."

Xieng Mieng smiled as two lovely young girls from the kingdom placed two gold necklaces around his neck.

Then he dipped his hand into the paint bowl and walked over to Khamsone's painting. He dragged his fingers down the painting.

"Mr. Khamsone, I have given your peacock five worms to nibble on."

THE KING OF THE JUNGLE

"Who is the king of the jungle?" asked the tiger as he sauntered through the tall grass.

"You, of course," said the rabbit.

"You are the king of the jungle," said the deer.

"Everyone knows that the tiger is the king of the jungle," said the crocodile.

"The tiger is the king," said the owl. "The tiger fears no animal."

The tiger smiled proudly and roared. "You are all correct. I, the tiger, am the king of the jungle. And don't you forget it."

But on that very same day, in that very same jungle, came a small animal. This small animal looked like a frog, hopped like a frog, and snagged flies just like a frog. But it was not a frog. This animal was ugly with big brown bumps all over its back.

It was a toad. The toad was in a big hurry. It was chasing a juicy fly. Unfortunately, the toad did not notice the tiger and the toad just hopped right in front of him.

"Do you not know who I am?" roared the tiger. "I am the king of the jungle. You have crossed my path. Are you not afraid of the king of the jungle?"

"Oh, hello, Mr. Tiger. I didn't see you. Am I afraid of you? Why should I be afraid of you?"

"Because I am the king of the jungle and all animals are afraid of me. I can kill you with one swing of my paw."

"Ha ha," laughed the toad. "I am not afraid of you. I ate a tiger yesterday. It was delicious. It looked just like you. Do you have a brother?"

"You ate a tiger?" asked the tiger with surprise.

"Yes, I didn't eat the bones, just the meat. Tiger meat is quite tasty," said the toad as he licked his toad lips with his long toad tongue.

"You ate a tiger?" asked the tiger in amazement.

"Yes, it was recommended by my doctor. I try to eat a tiger at least once a week. Tiger meat is good for my health. It puts a bounce in my hop."

"You ate a tiger?" asked the tiger with alarm.

"Yes, I do so once or twice a week. Now, I don't mean to be rude but I am in a bit of a hurry. It was nice chatting with you. Now go back into the jungle and eat plenty of animals and get nice and fat. Come back next week. I should be hungry by then. It was nice meeting you."

The toad turned around and hopped away through the tall grass.

The tiger stood in shock.

A few moments later, the tiger was startled by a noise in the trees above. A monkey was jumping from limb to limb.

"Hey, monkey, come down here. I have a question for you."

"Yes, King Tiger, what could that question be?"

"Do you think that it is possible for a toad to eat a tiger?"

"Hee, hee, hee, ha, ha, ha, hee, hee, hee," laughed the monkey. "You must be joking. Toads don't eat tigers. Toads eat flies."

"But I met a toad and he said that he eats a tiger once a week."

"Do you believe that a tiny toad can eat a big tiger?

"Did the toad lie to me? Lie to the king of the jungle?"

"King Tiger, let's go find that toad. We will make him tell the truth. And then you can eat him for your snack."

"What if he is telling the truth? What if he really does eat tigers?"

"Toads don't eat tigers. But if you are worried we can tie our tails together."

So the monkey and the tiger tied their tails together and headed back into the jungle in search of the toad. Soon they found the animal with the big brown bumps on its back. It was the toad.

"There is our toad," said the monkey, "are you ready for your afternoon snack?"

"You talk to him," said the tiger. "Make him tell the truth."

"Hello, Mr. Toad. I hear that you have been saying some crazy things to our king of the jungle. Did you say that you eat tigers?"

"Hello, Mr. Monkey, thank you for coming. And thank you for bringing me another tiger to eat. This is the second tiger you have brought me. You promised to bring me five tigers. That means that you still must bring three more tigers. Okay, just put the tiger over there next to the tree."

"What?" roared the tiger. "Monkey, you lied to me! The toad is going to eat me!" The tiger leaped into the air and bounded through the forest.

But the tiger forgot that there was a monkey tied to his tail.

Bonk! The monkey's head hit a tree.

Crash! The monkey's legs hit a big rock.

Wham! The monkey's arms hit a clump of bamboo.

Clonk! The monkey's head hit another rock.

Finally, the tiger tired and stopped to rest under a tall tree. He noticed the monkey tied to his tail.

"So, monkey, you fear the toad too. Is the toad the king of the jungle after all?"

But the monkey was too dazed, and too hurt and too frightened to reply.

THE INTREPID TOAD

A few weeks later, in that same jungle, the very same monkey was arguing with a different tiger.

"Jump? We tigers can jump very high. Do you see that tall tree? My father could jump higher than that," said the tiger.

"Hee, hee, hee, ha, ha, ha, hee, hee, hee," laughed the monkey. "Do you see that big fluffy cloud? My grandfather could jump up to a cloud and bring it back down to earth. He used the cloud as a pillow."

"Hah!" scoffed the tiger. "Have you seen the moon at night? My great-grandfather liked to read. Since there was not enough light at night to read, he would jump to the moon and read by its light."

"Do you see the sun?" said the monkey pointing to the big red ball in the morning sky. "My great-great-grandfather liked roasted bananas for breakfast. So he would jump up to the sun and the sun would roast his bananas."

"Okay, then, Mr. Monkey. Let's see how high you can jump. Let's have us a jumping contest. Just the two of us. Then we will see who can jump the highest."

Fine," said the monkey. "Let's have a jumping contest. When?"

"Now."

"Not yet," said the monkey. "I haven't had my breakfast yet. I'm going to eat some bananas." And the monkey jumped up into the trees and swung through the forest to search for some ripe bananas.

"Excuse me, Mr. Tiger," said a voice buried in the thick jungle grass. "I can jump higher than you."

The tiger brushed aside the tall grass to find the toad.

"You, a little toad, can jump higher than me? Don't make me laugh!"

"Laugh all you want, Mr. Tiger, but I can jump higher than you. I challenge you to a jumping contest. Right here, right now."

"Not now, Toad. I am busy."

"You're not busy. You are afraid. You are afraid that I will beat you."

"Afraid of losing a jumping contest to an ugly little toad? Don't make me laugh."

"If you don't want to have a jumping contest with me, then you are afraid."

"All right, toad. Let's have our jumping contest."

The tiger swung his tail to the ground to get ready for his jump. When the tiger's tail hit the ground the toad opened his tiny toad mouth and chomped down hard on the tiger's tail with his toad teeth.

"YEOW!" yelled the tiger as he jumped and swung his tail high into the air. The toad let go of the tiger's tail and flew up above the tiger, above the tree and back to the ground.

"You bit my tail!"

"I did. And I jumped higher than you, didn't I?"

"You tricked me."

"Maybe. But I did jump higher than you."

"You tricked me. You bit my tail and now it hurts. Toad, I am going to the forest to find some medicine."

Just a few minutes after the tiger went to search for some medicine, the monkey returned.

"Oh, no. It's you again. What are you doing here, Mr. Toad? Have you come to watch the jumping match between me and Mr. Tiger?"

"The jumping contest has to be cancelled."

"Why?"

"Because the tiger is no more. I ate him."

" Hee, hee, hee, ha, ha, ha, hee, hee, hee," laughed the monkey. "Don't lie to me. You can fool a stupid tiger but you can't fool a wise monkey. Toads do not eat tigers."

"Yes we do. You don't believe me? Look what is in my mouth." The toad opened his mouth wide.

The monkey bent down and looked into the toad's mouth. Much to the monkey's surprise he saw fur and blood.

"Do you see the fur?"

"Yes."

"That fur is tiger fur."

"Hmm. It does look like tiger fur," admitted the monkey.

"Do you see blood?"

"Yes, I do."

"That blood is tiger blood."

"Hmm. It does look like tiger blood. Did you really eat that tiger?"

"I did. But I am still hungry. I think I shall eat a monkey."

"No!" screamed the monkey. "Don't eat me!"

The monkey jumped high into the tree and swung from branch to branch deep into the jungle.

THE KING LOSES HIS APPETITE

"I'm just not in the mood to eat," said the king.

All was not well in the palace. The cooks were beside themselves with worry. They had prepared the most scrumptious, delectable, delicious, appetizing dishes but the king took nary a bite.

They brought platters of the king's favorite foods; barbecued chicken, beef *laap*, roasted pork, red ant egg soup. When these dishes grew cold, they were replaced with freshly cooked ones. But the king didn't even give them a glance.

"I'm just not hungry," said the king with a sigh. "Someone must know how to restore my appetite."

"That someone is me," said Xieng Mieng. "I know an herb that is guaranteed to bring back appetite."

"What herb is that?" asked the king.

"It is the leaf of a special tree that grows deep within the forest.

"Take one of my guards with you and bring it back as soon as possible. Go now!"

"I wish that it were that easy. Unfortunately, this herb only works if the leaf is eaten immediately after it is plucked from the tree. Do not worry, Your Majesty. I will take you there myself. We will go tomorrow. We will leave the palace at the break of dawn. Please ask the royal cooks to prepare some food for me for the journey."

The next morning the king and Xieng Mieng headed out for the hills. Xieng Mieng carried a basket filled with sticky rice and barbecued chicken cooked in the royal kitchen.

"It smells wonderful," said Xieng Mieng.

They walked through the rice fields, through the bamboo forests and into the cool foothills.

"Are we there yet?" asked the king.

"No, we have a long way to go," answered Xieng Mieng.

They continued walking up the path as the sun rose in the sky.

The king, who didn't get much exercise, was huffing and puffing. He took every chance he got to drink water from the cool mountain stream that flowed next to their path. He was actually beginning to feel a tingle in his stomach, a feeling he recognized as something close to hunger.

The sun reached the top of the sky. "Are we there yet?"

"Not yet," said Xieng Mieng. "We are still a long way from finding the tree with the special leaf. This long walk has made me quite hungry."

Xieng Mieng and the king sat down under the cool shade of a monkey pod tree. Xieng Mieng dipped into the basket and took out a meaty chicken leg.

"I'll have one too," said the king.

"No you won't. You cannot eat anything before you eat the leaf from the tree. If you do it the herb will lose its effect and your appetite will not come back."

Xieng Mieng pulled the meat from the chicken bone and gobbled it down. "Yummy! This is the tastiest barbecued chicken I have had for a long time. Yummy!" Xieng Mieng smacked his lips as he tossed the chicken bone into the forest. As a finishing touch, he uttered a deep and satisfying belch.

"You have excellent cooks in the royal kitchen. It is a pity that you can't have any food. Oh, well, we had better get going if we are going to find that tree."

Xieng Mieng and the king resumed their trek into the hills.

As they hiked deeper into the forest the king became more and more hungry. He searched the trees that gave the travelers shade for fruit. He searched the vines that lined the path for berries.

"Xieng Mieng, I am hungry. I want the rest of the chicken," demanded the king.

"I am very sorry. If you eat now you will have no hope of getting back your appetite. It will mean that this long trek will have been for nothing. Don't think about that delicious barbecued chicken. If you think about that tasty chicken it will just make you hungrier."

They walked on.

"Ohhh!" groaned Xieng Mieng.

"What's the matter?" asked the king.

"It's nothing. I'm fine." Then a few minutes later he groaned again. This time even louder.

"Xieng Mieng, tell me what is the problem."

"Your Majesty, my shoulder hurts." Xieng Mieng put the basket down and massaged his shoulder.

"I'll carry the basket for a while," offered the king.

"Oh no, I couldn't let you do that. You would be tempted to eat the chicken."

"I will carry it until your shoulder feels better."

"All right. Don't think about the barbecued chicken in the basket. And try not to smell the delicious aroma."

The king hoisted the basket on his shoulder and they continued on their way.

The scent of the barbecued chicken was powerful and the king's hunger became like an angry animal in his stomach.

"Let's rest a moment," said the king.

But as soon as he had taken the basket off his shoulder he found that his hand had yanked out a leg of barbecued chicken and had stuffed it into his mouth.

"Don't eat that chicken!" said Xieng Mieng

But the king had already taken many bites and soon devoured the whole chicken leg.

"So, Your Majesty, now you understand that the best herb for eating is hunger. Every day you have so much food on your table that you have never really known hunger. Now you know hunger and now your appetite is back."

The king was furious with Xieng Mieng. But he was more hungry than angry and he finished off the rest of the chicken and a basket filled with sticky rice.

THE KING'S CAT

With big green eyes and soft snow-white fur, the king's cat was a strikingly beautiful animal. The king was very proud of his cat. It had won many contests and the king saw to it that the cat had the best of everything.

The king assigned a cook to prepare the tastiest of dishes—fresh fish, chicken in gravy, barbecued mouse. And each meal was served in a bowl of solid gold.

Nothing was too good for this cat. Some citizens grumbled about the amount of attention the king paid to the cat.

Xieng Mieng decided to teach the king a lesson.

Late one night, Xieng Mieng crept into the grounds of the king's palace. He carried a fat tasty mouse with a long string attached to his tail. Xieng Mieng spied the cat scampering across the long veranda.

Xieng Mieng tossed the mouse onto the veranda.

"Eek eek eek," shrieked the mouse.

The king's cat chased after the mouse. Xieng Mieng tugged the mouse's tail and the cat followed the mouse right into Xieng Mieng's outstretched arms.

"You have a new home now, cat," said Xieng Mieng.

"Meow," said the cat as Xieng Mieng carried the cat back to his house.

The next morning the cat was hungry. "Meow, meow, meow," it cried.

Xieng Mieng set out two bowls. One bowl was a lovely gold bowl filled with fresh fish. The other bowl was made from simple clay and was filled with leftover rice and a few table scraps.

The cat dashed for the gold bowl.

Whap! Xieng Mieng hit the cat

"Meow!" cried the cat. The cat tried to grab the fish.

Whap!

"Meow!" The cat tried again.

But Xieng Mieng hit him again.

"Meow! Meow!" yelled the cat. But each time the cat tried to seize a bit of fish from the golden bowl, Xieng Mieng hit him with the stick.

Finally, the cat, tired and hungry, walked to the simple clay bowl. He sniffed the rice. He sniffed again. He walked around the bowl. He walked around the bowl again.

He tasted the rice. Then he ran to the golden bowl.

Whap!

He returned to the clay bowl and finished off the rice.

"Good cat," said Xieng Mieng.

Each morning and each evening Xieng Mieng put out the two bowls: the golden bowl with fresh rice and the clay bowl with leftover rice. And each time the cat ran straight to the golden bowl. And each time he was hit with the stick.

After many days, the cat gave up and ran to the simple clay bowl and devoured the rice, ignoring the fresh fish in the golden bowl.

Meanwhile, the king was quite upset. The servants had looked high and low in the palace but could not find the cat.

The king called his royal guard. "As you know, my beautiful cat is missing. Search every square meter of this kingdom until you find it."

That very afternoon a guard came to Xieng Mieng's house. He saw the cat. It looked like a skinnier and dirtier version of the king's cat.

"Is that your cat?" asked the guard.

"It is," said Xieng Mieng.

"Meow," said the cat.

The guard looked closely at the cat and the closer he looked the more he was convinced that this cat was indeed the cat of the king. "This cat looks a lot like our king's cat. You are under arrest for stealing the king's cat. The cat and you must come with me to the palace."

"My cat, my beautiful cat," cried the king. "You are so thin, and so dirty. You need a bowl of fresh fish."

"Meow," said the cat.

"Your Majesty, this cat is not your cat. This is my cat," said Xieng Mieng. "I can prove it with a simple test."

"How?"

"Have your cooks fill your cat's golden bowl with fresh fish and put some leftover rice in my cat's simple clay bowl. If the cat is your cat, he will eat fish from the golden bowl, but if this cat is my cat he will eat rice from the clay bowl."

The two bowls were brought out. The cat looked at the king. The cat looked at the golden bowl. The cat looked at Xieng Mieng and then looked at the clay bowl.

He circled round the two bowls and sniffed at the fish. Then he glanced at Xieng Mieng.

He darted to the clay bowl and gulped down the rice.

"My cat is not impressed with a golden bowl or expensive food," said Xieng Mieng.

And when the cat had finished the bowl of rice, he took the cat and walked home.

THE TIGER RETIRES

A long time ago there was a beautiful forest with tall trees, wide rivers, and thick jungles filled with many different kinds of animals and birds. There were crocodiles and bears and deer and rabbits and squirrels and monkeys and snakes. And the king of these animals was, of course, the tiger.

One afternoon the tiger was resting under the shade of a broad banyan tree. Through the corner of his eye, he spied a deer running by.

"Dinner." The tiger leaped to his feet and tore after the deer.

Tigers are, generally, faster than deer. But these fast tigers are young and fit. This tiger was, unfortunately, old and fat. The deer realized he was being chased by the tiger and put on some speed. The tiger followed him in hot and hungry pursuit. But the tiger's legs began to hurt and he slowed down.

"Forget it!" said the tiger. "This running and chasing animals is just too difficult these days. I quit!"

The next day the tiger called a meeting of all the animals in the forest. All of the animals assembled in front of a cave at the edge of the jungle.

"As you know," the tiger began, "I am the king of the jungle. I have been a good king. Of course I have eaten some of your relatives but I must eat. Don't snakes eat mice? Don't crocodiles eat monkeys? Don't eagles eat rabbits?"

The animals gave each other nervous glances. Food was a very sensitive topic in the jungle. The monkeys moved far away from the crocodiles, the mice from the snake, the rabbits from the eagles.

"I don't eat a lot," continued the tiger. "Maybe a deer for dinner, or a snake for a snack. Actually, I don't ever remember eating snake." The tiger smacked his lips with the memory of some of his tastier meals. The deer hid behind a tree.

"But that is all over. I am getting old now and it is time for me to retire. I am going to go into that cave and I am going to meditate. Please, dear friends, try not to disturb me. But if you have an argument that you cannot decide, come to me. My eyes and legs may be a bit weak but my mind is still very strong. I can still be a good judge. And so, my friends, good-bye."

The tiger turned and walked slowly to the cave. "Good-bye, King Tiger, we will miss you . . ." they said as he walked into the cave.

". . . NOT!" And the animals cheered and laughed and danced and sang.

The animal that was dancing and singing the loudest was the rabbit. The rabbit lived in a cozy warm hole in a beautiful tree. One day the rabbit went out for a walk in the forest to look for some tasty turnips.

A partridge just happened to fly by and noticed the hole in the tree. As partridges live in tree holes this partridge was particularly excited to see a hole so cozy and warm. In fact, the hole was so cozy and so warm that the partridge decided to move in to the hole.

That afternoon the rabbit returned to the hole and hopped into his home.

"Aak!" yelled the partridge when the rabbit landed on his tummy. "Get off me!"

"Who are you?" yelled the rabbit. "Get out of my home!"

"It is my home now," said the partridge. "I have moved in here."

"It is my home," said the rabbit. "Now just get out!"

"No, you get off my stomach and get out of my house!"

"You get out!"

"No, you get out!"

The partridge and the rabbit argued and argued and argued.

"What is all the commotion about? You woke me up from a nap." It was a monkey who was snoozing in a branch at the top of the tree.

"I went out to find some food for my lunch and I come back to find that this squawking bird has moved into my house."

"It's my house now. I don't see a sign saying 'Rabbit's House.'"

"Every animal in this forest knows that this hole belongs to me. I don't need to put up . . ."

"Stop!" yelled the monkey. "If you can't work this out you must go see the old tiger who lives in the cave. He is fair. He will decide."

And so the partridge and the rabbit agreed to visit the old tiger in the cave.

"King Tiger, oh, King Tiger," called the rabbit into the mouth of the cave. "King Tiger, King Tiger?"

After a few minutes the tiger stumbled to the mouth of the cave to greet his guests. He rubbed the sleep from his eyes because he had just woken from a long nap.

"King Tiger, I am sorry that we woke you up. We have a problem. Can you help us?"

"Dear friends, of course I can help. That is what I am here to do. Now tell your king your problem."

"I lived in a cozy warm hole in a tree," began the rabbit, "and I went out to find some food for lunch and I came back to my hole to find that this miserable bird had moved in. I want my house back. It is mine."

"I was wandering through the forest and I found this empty hole in a tree," said the partridge. "There was no one there. I liked the hole and I decided to move in there. Finders keepers!"

"But it is my hole!" yelled the rabbit.

"My dear friends," said the tiger, "thank you for coming to me with your problem. Let me take a moment to consider this situation."

And the tiger closed his eyes for a moment and smiled.

"Yes, come here partridge, let me tell you my decision."

The partridge approached the tiger. The tiger swept the partridge into his paw and opened his jaws.

Crunch, crunch, crunch!

"Thank you, King Tiger," said the rabbit, "now I will go back and live in my hole."

"Thank you for bringing me this case. It was, actually, a very easy decision. You had the right to the hole. You had lived there first. Now aren't you going to thank me? Here, shake my paw."

And the happy rabbit hopped over to the tiger and shook his much larger paw.

The tiger grabbed the rabbit around the neck and opened his jaws.

Crunch, crunch, crunch!

"That was delicious," said the tiger. "I hope there will be more arguments in the jungle for me to settle."

THE LAST TRICK

Xieng Mieng continued to play tricks on the king and the king got angrier and angrier and angrier. Finally the king could take it no longer.

He called his royal guard.

"Xieng Mieng is always making me upset and angry. He is always making me look like a fool. He has caused me to lose face for the last time. We are like two tigers in a cage. Xieng Mieng must die."

The royal guard gasped. But in those days the king was the king. And the royal guards dared not disobey an order of the king. The king ordered the cook to mix poison into a bottle of honey and then he poured it into a beautiful ceramic jar.

That afternoon the king brought the jar to Xieng Mieng's house.

"Xieng Mieng, you have tricked me many times. I know now that you are cleverer than me. I have brought for you a jar of the tastiest honey in the kingdom. Drink this honey and enjoy the sweet taste of success."

"I'll have some now, won't you join me?" asked Xieng Mieng.

"No time. No time. I must take care of some other business. Enjoy the honey." The king rode back to the palace.

Xieng Mieng knew that the honey was poisoned. But he also knew that he had to drink it.

That evening he said a long good-bye to his wife.

The next morning he got ready to drink the honey.

"My dear wife. This is the morning that I must die. You must help me play my last trick. Here is what you must do. After I am dead just leave my body here in the rocking chair and pretend that I am still alive. Put these reading glasses on my face and prop my eyes open with these fishhooks. Put *The Vientiane Times* in my hands and a glass of hot tea on the table."

"What is that buzzing noise?" asked his wife.

"Ah, I've put a carpenter bee in this bamboo tube. Keep it under the table. Doesn't it sound like a person reading?"

Xieng Mieng laughed and smiled and gave a warm goodbye to his faithful patient wife and then he drank the honey.

Xieng Mieng passed away with a big smile on his lips.

Xieng Mieng's wife cried and cried and laughed and laughed when she remembered her difficult, unpredictable, and funny husband.

Xieng Mieng's wife did exactly as Xieng Mieng had instructed. She pulled up his eyelids and fastened fishhooks on his glasses to keep them open. She spread out a copy of *The Vientiane Times* (open to the cartoon page) and put it in his hands. And she poured a hot cup of tea in Xieng Mieng's cup.

Soon a soldier from the king's royal guard came to Xieng Mieng's house and knocked on the door.

"The king is inquiring about the jar of honey that he gave to Xieng Mieng. Did he enjoy it?"

"That is very kind of the king. You know that Xieng Mieng just loves honey. In fact, he ate almost the entire jar. You can ask him yourself. He is sitting in his rocking chair reading *The Vientiane Times*. He is drinking a cup of tea. Go see for yourself."

"What is that noise?"

"Oh, Xieng Mieng reads out loud. He never learned to read silently."

The guard saw Xieng Mieng sitting on his rocking chair reading *The Vientiane Times*.

"Would you care for a cup of tea? I think I can sweeten it with a bit of honey."

The guard stared at Xieng Mieng.

"Are you sure I cannot get you a cup of tea with this honey?"

"I must return to the palace."

"Then please take the king's ceramic jar back with you. And please thank him for the honey."

The soldier took the jar and ran back to the palace.

"What? He is still alive? He drank the entire bottle?" yelled the angry king. "There was enough poison in this jar to kill an elephant. Maybe the honey wasn't really poisoned?"

And then the king did something very foolish. Something that he would regret for the rest of his short life. He took a taste of the poisoned honey.

In a few minutes the poison began to do its work.

"Xieng Mieng! Your tricked me one last time!"

And the king died too.

Who knows? Maybe in their next lives, Xieng Mieng is still playing tricks on the king.

NOTES

Xieng Mieng Follows the King Exactly

The literality of words is mocked in this tale. Many Xieng Mieng stories use this deliberate misinterpretation or over-interpretation of words as the crux of the tale ("cross the river" in "How Xieng Mieng Got His Name."). This is also a swipe at formality of legal, academic and religious texts and how one can "lose the forest for the trees."

The Tragic Tale of the Flying Turtle

This tale makes much more sense when you understand that the word for underarm odor in Lao is *kee tao* (literally turtle excrement).

I have heard different versions of this tale throughout Southeast Asia. The tale told in Bali has an old man pointing to the flying swans and turtles and yelling "Look, the swans are carrying a piece of shit!"

It Tastes Sweet

Different regions of Laos and Thailand have different versions of the Xieng Mieng tales. In northern Laos and northern Thailand, the novice Kham is a character named Katampa. In this version, Katampa is one of three brothers: Katampa, Xieng Mieng and Puseth. The parents of these brothers were beggars who were once denied passage across a river by the king, an abbot and people of the Lua ethnic group. The parents raised their children to avenge this slight—Katampa bedevils the monks of the temple, Xieng Mieng torments the King and Puseth harasses the Lua.

The Bottle of Honey

In many Buddhist cultures there is a tradition of lampooning the foibles and weaknesses of monks. Notable examples of this tradition are the Japanese tales of widows seducing monks and Tibet's hilarious (and often X-rated) Uncle Tompa tales.

The anger of the abbot in this tale is particularly striking in a culture which prizes the value of patience and restraint, *chai yen* (literally a "cool heart").

How Xieng Mieng Got His Name

In Thailand, Xieng Mieng is known as Sithanonchai, sometimes written Si Thanonchai. In Northeast Thailand (known as Isaan) most of the 20 million population can speak Lao and the character is known both as Xieng Mieng and Sithanonchai. Achan Kanyarat Vechasat of Mahidol University traces the Xieng Mieng tales in the region in *Srithanonchai in Southeast Asia* (written in Thai).

The Tug of War

The Giant Mekong Catfish (*Pangasianodon gigas*) can weigh as much as 300 kilograms (650 pounds) and grow to a length of 3 meters (10 feet). It is critically endangered.

The *kataw* is a small ball woven from rattan that is either kicked or headed in a *kataw* game. It is called *takraw* in Thailand.

The Bird that Spoke Five Languages Fluently

Some readers may be surprised by the cruelty towards animals. But in Laos, birds and animals are considered animate edibles. When I lived in Laos a prominent animal conservation organization sent interviewers out to survey inhabitants who lived in or near a projected national wildlife protection zones. They presented interviewees with photographs of the animals that lived in the area to document the frequency of encounters. The interviewers were inevitably advised on favorite recipes for the identified animal. Hunting in Laos is a favorite activity and considered, in many areas, essential to the local diet.

The Lion's Lunch

This popular tale can be found in both Aesop's fables and the Panchatantra tales.

Speed vs. Cunning

It is easy to see why the Pathet Lao popularized this particular tale. The collective power and detailed organization of the masses overpower an arrogant and seemingly undefeatable opponent.

I showed my *metta* (compassion) towards the rabbit in this tale by allowing him to slink away in shame. The Lao version has him die of exhaustion. I exercised the storyteller's option by disney-fying the tale. But, after all, wasn't Walt Disney a storyteller too?

Dr. Wajuppa Tossa of Mahasarakham University presents a different version of this tale in an outstanding website (www.seasite. niu.edu/lao/laofolkliterature/chapter5/chapter5_text.htm)

In this version Xieng Mieng has the role of the rabbit. Interestingly, Dr. Brenges (*Revue Indochinese*, 1904, p. 844) records the same tale but in his telling the rabbit is named Xieng Mieng.

The King Tries to Trick Xieng Mieng

This is the best known Xieng Mieng tale in Laos. If you ask most Lao to tell you a Xieng Mieng tale, this will likely be the tale. However, if you ask a Thai to tell a Sithanonchai tale, you are likely to hear the story of how Sithanonchai kills his brother. Though written Lao versions of Xieng Mieng include this story I never once heard this tale in Laos. Could it be that the Pathet Lao did not want to sully the character of Xieng Mieng with fratricide and excised this tale?

Three Friendly Flies

I have not been able to determine the roots to this tale. I suspect that this may have been written by the Pathet Lao to dramatize the differences between the aristocracy, merchant class and the common man.

The health message of brushing one's teeth is my addition. Political and health messages were often added by the storyteller to further his or her own agenda.

The King Loses His Appetite

Note how Xieng Mieng chastises the king for "not knowing hunger." In this tale, the storyteller is indicting the rulers for not feeling the pain of the people.

The Tiger Retires

This tale was told to me by a student at the Lao School of Law.

The Last Trick

Though it was rarely exercised, the king had the power of life and death over his subjects.

9 789749 575871